Who Runs This Country, Anyway?

A Guide to Canadian Government

Written and illustrated by

Joanne Stanbridge

Cover illustration by Lorna Bennett

Scholastic Canada Ltd.
Toronto New York London Auckland Sydney
Mexico City New Delhi Hong Kong Buenos Aires

Scholastic Canada Ltd.
175 Hillmount Road, Markham, Ontario L6C 1Z7, Canada

Scholastic Inc.
555 Broadway, New York, NY 10012, USA

Scholastic Australia Pty Limited
PO Box 579, Gosford, NSW 2250, Australia

Scholastic New Zealand Limited
Private Bag 94407, Greenmount, Auckland, New Zealand

Scholastic Ltd.
Villiers House, Clarendon Avenue, Leamington Spa,
Warwickshire CV32 5PR, UK

Library and Archives Canada Cataloguing in Publication
Stanbridge, Joanne, 1960-
Who runs this country, anyway? : a guide to Canadian
government / Joanne Stanbridge.

ISBN 0-439-94763-4 (bound).--ISBN 0-439-95730-3 (pbk)

1. Canada—Politics and government—Juvenile literature.
2. Federal government—Canada—Juvenile literature. I. Title.

JL75.S83 2005   j320.471   C2005-900638-27

6 5 4 3 2 1   Printed in Canada   05 06 07 08 09

Table of Contents

*To Peter Milliken's staff in Kingston
and on Parliament Hill. They opened my eyes to
government at its best: informative, efficient
and warmly welcoming. Many thanks.*

INTRODUCTION:

Quiet on the Set!

All week our classmates have been telling us about important topics like *Bike Manufacturing in Eastern Ontario* and *The Life Cycle of the Sea Urchin*. But today we — Zoe and Nathan — are going to tell you about something even more important. Our topic is *The Canadian Government.*

No, stop! Don't run away!

Our talk will be short. It will be easy to understand. And it won't be boring. Honest. By the time we're done, you'll know more about Canadian government than the average adult.

You'll be able to talk like this:

ADULT: Thanks to those jokers in Ottawa, I'll be paying more tax this year. Who runs this country, anyway?

YOU: Actually, the prime minister and cabinet introduce most of the bills, which must pass through both the House of Commons and the Senate. So technically **they** are running the country.

ADULT: Whuh . . . ?

YOU: On the other hand, if the government can't get enough support for an important bill, it could fall on a vote of non-confidence.

ADULT: Pardon?

YOU: Then we'd have to go back to the polls. Well . . . **you** would, anyway. I'm too young to vote.

Thanks to us, you'll be able amaze and impress the adults in your life. When they talk nonsense, you can correct them. Best of all, when you grow up you can run the country yourself. Now that's what we call fun. Sit back and listen. We'll tell you how to do it.

CHAPTER 1

TAKE ME TO YOUR LEADER

Don't be scared of the word government. The government is just a bunch of people who speak for the rest of us. There are more than 30 million people in Canada. We can't all go to Ottawa to run the country (whew . . . wouldn't *that* be a party?) so each community chooses one person to represent it.

We say these people are running the country, but since we're the ones who choose them, *we* — the millions of ordinary Canadians — are really running the country. This kind of government, where ordinary people choose other ordinary people to speak for them, is called a representative democracy.

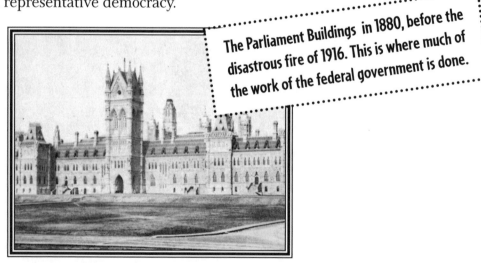

The Parliament Buildings in 1880, before the disastrous fire of 1916. This is where much of the work of the federal government is done.

Nathan says he's not an ordinary person. (No kidding.) But when I say ordinary, I mean that in Canada nobody has a special right to lead us. Nathan can't fight his way to power like an army general, or be born to it like a king. In a democracy, everybody has an equal right to vote and to try to be elected.

As an ordinary person, you can tell the government what to do. You can keep an eye on it by watching the news. You can make sure the people who speak for you know what you want. You can tell them what you think, write letters or e-mails, march in protests, sign petitions or join organizations. You can do these things even if you didn't vote for the person who represents your community. You can do them even if you're not old enough to vote yet. As an added bonus, if you're over 18 and a Canadian citizen, you can also vote in elections, become a Member of Parliament, or even be the prime minister. Being an ordinary person is your first step toward running the country. Congratulations! You're already on your way to the top!

Nathan says he'll start by being a mayor. See how mixed up he is? Sometimes you'll hear an adult making the same mistake, so pay attention. This could be your chance to show off!

Before you start running the country, you need to know that there are three different kinds of government in Canada: municipal government, provincial/territorial government, and federal government. Won't the adults in your life be impressed when you start using those big words? To find out how, turn the page!

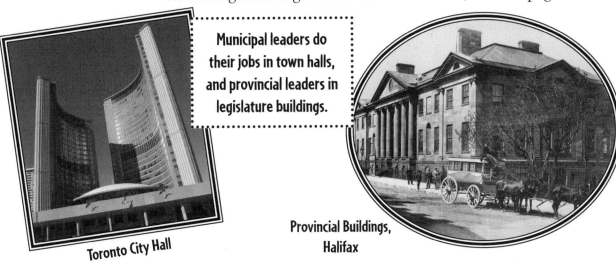

Municipal leaders do their jobs in town halls, and provincial leaders in legislature buildings.

Toronto City Hall

Provincial Buildings, Halifax

Municipal Government

A government that runs a city, town, village, county or region is called a municipal government. There are about 4000 of these in Canada. They're in charge of local matters such as streets and sidewalks, police and fire departments, garbage and sewage disposal, parks and swimming pools, ice rinks and libraries. The people in your municipal government are usually called city councillors, reeves or aldermen, and the person in charge is the mayor. When you get old enough, you'll vote for these people in a special election (called a municipal election). They run your city. They don't run Canada. See the difference?

Provincial/Territorial Government

Nathan wants more power. Maybe he could run a province or territory. As you know, there are thirteen of these. Each of them has a person in charge, called a premier, and a bunch of members. The government of a province or territory works almost exactly the same way as the government of Canada, which often causes adults to mix them up — but *you* can tell the difference.

For one thing, the provincial or territorial government is only allowed to make decisions about provincial or territorial matters. So if you hear someone mention hospitals, schools or electricity, they're usually talking about the provincial/territorial government, *not* the Canadian government.

To be extra-sure, find out what the members are called. There's a tiny difference in the words that are used for them. You have to listen carefully to hear it! The people who run the country are called Members of Parliament (MPs, for short). But the people who run provinces and territories have an extra word in their titles, like this:

🍁 In most provinces and territories, they're called Members of the Legislative Assembly (MLAs).

* In Quebec, they're called Members of the National Assembly (MNAs).
* In Ontario, they're called Members of Provincial Parliament (MPPs).
* In Newfoundland, they're called Members of the House of Assembly (MHAs).

This is where the fun starts. If you listen closely, you're almost sure to hear an adult getting confused between the people who are running the country and those who are running your province or territory. Just smile sweetly and correct them. They'll be sure to thank you. Heh-heh.

See? We told you this would be fun.

Federal Government

Uh-oh. Now Nathan wants to be the prime minister. He wants to be the head of the government in Ottawa, the one that runs the whole country. It's called the federal government, and it's in charge of things that cross from one province or territory into another, like airlines, banks, armies and broadcasting. It's also in charge of things that reach beyond our borders, like immigration, and whether we're friends or enemies with other countries.

The federal government is huge. It's divided into three branches:

1. the legislative branch, which makes new laws and fixes (or gets rid of) old laws
2. the executive branch, which makes sure the laws are carried out, or "executed," (No, Nathan, not that kind of execution! Good grief!) and spends our tax money
3. the judicial branch, where judges in courtrooms interpret and apply the laws.

Together, the first two branches are called Parliament. But the judicial branch is separate from them, and it's *not* part of Parliament. We'll tell you why in a moment.

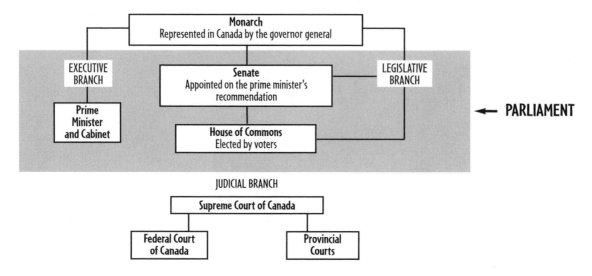

Parliament

When adults talk about "the people who run this country," they're almost always talking about the Members of Parliament (MPs) who have been chosen by ordinary Canadians from across the country, and sent to Ottawa. There are more than 300 of these members. The place where they meet is called the House of Commons, but it's not a house and it's not common. It's a very special room — so special that only the people who work there are allowed to walk on its floor. Visitors have to sit in balconies near the ceiling!

Down the hall from the House of Commons is another room called the Senate. The people who work there are called senators. There are more than 100 of them. They're chosen by the prime minister. Once they become senators, they get to stay in their jobs until they retire at the age of 75. Most of them have had important careers — for example, as mayors, MPs, judges, professors or presidents of large companies — before they became senators. Some people think senators should be elected instead of appointed, but so far that hasn't happened.

If you ask an adult what a senator does, the adult will probably laugh. That's partly because it's fashionable to make jokes about the Senate and partly because the adult doesn't exactly *know* what a senator does. But *you* will. Here's a handy list:

1. Senators study every law that's proposed by the House of Commons. They can change or reject a law if they think it might be harmful.
2. They can also propose certain types of new laws.
3. They study important issues like crime or health care and suggest improvements.
4. They speak up for minority groups who might not have a chance to make their points in the busy House of Commons. The Senate has been called the "house of sober second thought" because it reviews important issues so carefully.

It's the Law

Laws are the most important tool for running our country, and Parliament's main job is to make new laws. The branches of government that make new laws are the legislative and executive branches. (Nathan says he actually knew that! As soon as he finishes his victory dance, we can continue.)

The main job of the government's other branch — the judicial branch — is to interpret and apply the laws. Judges in courtrooms make decisions about how federal laws should be applied — for example, laws about copyright, citizenship or taxes. They help the government to interpret Canada's Constitution. They handle disputes between provinces, or between the provinces and the federal government. And they make decisions about important cases that have been appealed through the lower courts in the country.

The Rule of Law

People sometimes say "rules are made to be broken," but in Canada one rule is so important it cannot be broken. It's called the rule of law. It means that Canada's laws apply to everyone in the whole country. Nobody, not even the tiniest baby, is outside the protection of the law. And nobody, not even a powerful person like the prime minister, is allowed to break the law.

But if the judges and courts work *for* the government, how can they enforce the rule of law? Picture this:

JUDGE: Prime Minister, you broke the law. Go to prison.
PRIME MINISTER: No way. You're fired!

Luckily, that sort of scenario can't happen. The judges and courts that make up the judicial branch of government are kept strictly separate from Parliament. The prime minister has to respect the court's decisions. He or she can't fire the judges. This important rule is called the independence of the judiciary.

The Supreme Court

Our highest court is called the Supreme Court of Canada. Its nine judges help the government to interpret laws and apply them to real-life situations. It answers difficult questions such as "Can a teenager say *no* to a medical treatment that could save her life?" or "Can a province choose not to be part of Canada anymore?" The Supreme Court also listens to appeals from people who aren't satisfied with decisions made by the lower courts. When that happens, the Supreme Court's decision is final.

The nine justices of the Supreme Court help the government decide questions of law that affect all Canadians, or that the lower courts have not been able to agree on. (Nathan is impressed that their robes are bright red and trimmed with white fur.)

The Prime Minister

The prime minister is the head of government and the most powerful person in Canadian politics. He or she has been called "a moon among minor stars" and "first among equals." (Nathan, please take off that cape. The prime minister does not actually have superpowers.)

If you were the prime minister you'd have to listen carefully to everyone's opinions and do a good job of representing the people who elected you. You'd want to stay in power, so you'd work hard to keep the confidence of your colleagues and the ordinary Canadians they represent. And you'd want to keep being the prime minister after the next election too, so you couldn't just go around doing whatever you pleased. But if you were the prime minister and you felt strongly about an issue, your opinion could become Canada's official policy. In public, your advisors would have to agree with you. If they didn't, they would have to resign. Few people in Canada have that kind of power.

When Lester B. Pearson was a student, years before he became Canada's prime minister in 1963, he played hockey for Oxford University. That's him at the right.

HIRING POWER

The prime minister has the power to choose his or her own team of advisors and to fire them if necessary. The prime minister and his or her team also appoint Supreme Court judges. And the PM chooses more than 3000 other executives to work at various federal government jobs and agencies — agencies such as Canada Post or the Canadian Broadcasting Corporation (CBC). But don't worry, the prime minister doesn't have to do all this hiring alone! An excellent staff will be there to help.

The Governor General

If Nathan were the prime minister, could anyone say no to him? Luckily, yes. If he stepped too far out of line, the governor general could overrule him. This almost never happens, but in 1926 when our prime minister asked the governor general to end a session of parliament, the governor general said no because he thought the current session could survive a bit longer. It did — but only for four days! (If *Nathan* were the prime minister, the governor general would certainly have his or her hands full.)

Every five years a new governor general is chosen. The prime minister gets to do the choosing, and the Monarch then appoints the chosen person to the job. Imagine being able to tell the queen what to do!

The governor general has a ceremonial role, doing things like opening a new session of Parliament, delivering the government's Speech from the Throne, giving official approval to new laws, making sure that Canada always has a prime minister, and being the commander-in-chief of the armed forces. The governor general also does diplomatic work — travelling inside and outside Canada as a representative of our government, participating in ceremonies like Remembrance Day and Canada Day, meeting with important visitors to Canada, and giving awards to outstanding Canadians. How many of these duties can your favourite adults remember? (Feel free to give them a pop quiz!)

Governor General Adrienne Clarkson shakes the hand of a new Canadian citizen.

The Monarch

The official head of the Canadian government is the king or queen of Great Britain. Sometimes we call this person the Monarch, the Crown or the Sovereign. His or her powers are represented in Canada by the governor general, except during a royal visit. When the Monarch is in Canada, he or she has the right to perform those duties.

Every new law in Canada begins with the words: "Her Majesty, by and with the advice and consent of the Senate and the House of Commons, enacts as follows . . ."

But how did that happen? Why do we have a monarch?

Huge crowds turned out for the 2005 visit of Her Majesty Queen Elizabeth II to Saskatchewan and Alberta. (Nathan wants to know how many hats the Queen owns.)

CHAPTER 2

WHY DO WE HAVE A MONARCH?

Before Confederation

Long before Canada was a country, Great Britain was ruled by kings and queens. In fact, some of the early settlers from Great Britain and other countries in Europe came to North America because they didn't *like* their kings and queens — they wanted to get away from them! When these people first arrived they settled in British, French, Dutch and Spanish colonies, on land which had been home to First Nations people for thousands of years. Wars were fought and treaties were signed until finally Britain controlled almost all of the colonies. Then some of the colonies turned around and fought to be free of Britain, as well. They won their freedom and joined together into a new country called the United States of America (U.S.A.). The colonies to the north of them remained British and continued to be ruled by British kings and queens.

In the mid-1860s, the United States weren't exactly united. They were fighting a terrible war among themselves. It was called the Civil War but there was nothing civil about it — it was a nightmare. Some of the Canadian provinces to the north decided that they would be stronger if they were united, so they joined together into a new country called The Dominion of Canada.

FEDERALISM

The new country had four provinces: New Brunswick, Nova Scotia,
Ontario and Quebec. Each province got to keep its own government
and to control things that were inside its borders, such as schools and
roads. But the federal government took care of things that were
common to all of the provinces, like railways and trade agreements.
This system — where states or provinces have their own powers but are
also united under one central government — is called federalism.
It's also used in Switzerland, Australia and the United States.

The British North America Act

If you want to have a little fun, ask an adult what the *BNA Act* is. If he or she says it has something to do with cattle diseases, please do not laugh out loud. Just nod sympathetically. *BNA Act* stands for the *British North America Act*, which was written by the leaders of the colonies that formed The Dominion of Canada. It's the document that created Canada. In 1982 the document's name was changed to the *Constitution Act, 1867*. (Spring that on your favourite uncle — bet he won't know it!) But no matter what it was called, it set out the basic rules of Canadian government:

- ❦ It created Canadian provinces and brought them together under a federal government.
- ❦ It listed the powers of the federal and provincial governments.
- ❦ It made the Monarch the head of the Canadian government.
- ❦ It gave the provincial governments the right to change their own constitutions.
- ❦ But it didn't give the federal government the right to change its Constitution.

Now, tuck those facts into a corner of your brain and wait for a chance to recite them in front of a grown-up. (Nathan says this works even better in front of a group of grown-ups.) Look humble while you do it.

CANADA'S CONSTITUTION

If you really want to shine, remind your teacher that Canada is a constitutional monarchy. Even the Monarch's powers are limited by our country's Constitution. The Constitution is a set of rules that tells how our country's government will be run. It's made up of more than twenty-five written documents that were collected over time, plus some very important traditions that aren't written down anywhere. For example, it doesn't say anywhere in our Constitution that the prime minister is the head of our government. (Yes, Nathan, that's really true.) But don't worry! These unwritten traditions are just as strong as written laws.

Did you know that the name "House of Commons" comes from the term "commoners" — that's us, the ordinary people who elect the prime minister and the MPs who help run our country.

Confederation

Why mess with perfection? That's what the people who wrote the *BNA Act* thought. For hundreds of years their government had worked pretty well, so why not use the same system in Canada? That's why the newborn Canada looked very much like its British parent. Canada was loyal to the king or queen of Britain, and it had its own central government.

In Britain, two groups of advisors had always helped the king or queen. The first group represented the rich and powerful people — the lords. The second group represented the "common" people. Over time, the kings, queens and lords held less and less of the real power. More and more of Britain's decisions were made in the House of Commons, which represented the ordinary people.

Canada followed this tradition. It created its own House of Commons and its own Senate (which is the Canadian version of the British House of Lords).

When was Canada born? Your favourite adult might actually be able to answer this question, so make sure you know it too. Canada's

In 1864, in Charlottetown, P.E.I., leaders began the meetings that would result in the **BNA Act**. Note the fancy top hats.

birthday is called Confederation. It happened when the *BNA Act* was signed into law on July 1, 1867. Canada's new government began to meet in the Parliament Buildings in Ottawa. It has been meeting there ever since.

Gradually, the baby Canada started to grow up. Like a preteen and then a teenager, it became more and more independent. First it signed treaties without asking Britain for permission. Then, in the 1920s, our government decided we would not automatically send soldiers into conflicts in which the British were involved. The British were not amused.

At one meeting in London, our prime minister refused to say that Canada *must* do whatever Britain asked. Quietly and stubbornly, he convinced the others at the meeting: India, South Africa, New Zealand, Australia and Britain. Soon the countries formed a new kind of partnership called a Commonwealth. Each country was still loyal to Britain, but now each was free to make all its own decisions. Canada was growing up!

In 1867, leaders from four provinces decided how to unite as The Dominion of Canada. John A. Macdonald, Canada's first prime minister, is standing (hatless) before the central window.

The Constitution Act, 1982

Only one thing kept Canada from being totally independent of Britain. (No, Nathan, I don't mean a driver's licence.) If we wanted to change our Constitution we still had to ask for permission. In 1927, Canadians started trying to change that rule. It took over 54 years to work out the details! The provinces, territories and federal government argued and argued because they couldn't agree on the rules.

Finally an agreement was reached: the *Constitution Act, 1982*. This new act allowed Canada to change its own Constitution without asking permission from Britain. This was called patriation or "bringing the Constitution home." Like many agreements, it didn't satisfy everybody. Plenty of issues were (and are!) still being debated.

Want to have a little fun? Ask a grown-up what patriation is. If he or she knows the answer, assign 10 points. If he or she says "something to do with the Constitution," assign 5 points. If he or she says "Go walk the dog," assign 0 points and don't ask any more questions for a while.

Her Majesty Queen Elizabeth II signs the **Constitution Act, 1982**, as Prime Minister Pierre Elliott Trudeau (left) looks on.

ASSEMBLY OF
FIRST NATIONS

After the **Constitution Act** was signed in 1982, the prime minister
and premiers began to hold meetings with leaders from the
Assembly of First Nations to talk about Aboriginal
rights and concerns. These meetings are still going on.
The Assembly of First Nations represents more than 630 First Nations
communities in Canada. Its leaders meet once a year with hundreds of
chiefs to make plans and policies. Every three years, the assembly elects
a national chief, who is assisted by six vice-chiefs from different
regions of the country. The national chief is the official
spokesperson for First Nations people.

Phil Fontaine, one of the
leaders of the Assembly of
First Nations, and the
Assembly's logo.

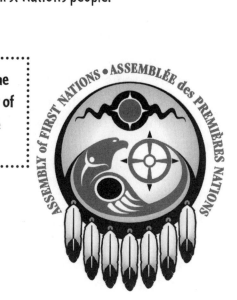

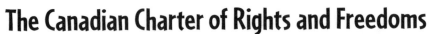

The Canadian Charter of Rights and Freedoms

The *Constitution Act, 1982* turned a very important document into law. You've probably heard of it: the *Canadian Charter of Rights and Freedoms*. It's a key part of the Constitution.

The *Charter* guarantees fundamental freedoms. It says that Canadians are free to follow their own beliefs, express their opinions, and meet with anybody they choose. These are called freedoms of conscience, religion, thought, expression, peaceful assembly and association. (Pardon? No, Nathan, "freedom from homework" is not guaranteed in the *Charter*.)

The *Canadian Charter of Rights and Freedoms* also guarantees Canadians' rights:

* democratic rights: for example, citizens have the right to vote in provincial and federal elections
* mobility rights, which include the right to move freely in and out of Canada and to go anywhere inside its borders
* legal rights, which mean the authorities can't search Canadians, seize their belongings, arrest or detain them unless the authorities can make a strong case to show someone has broken the law (and if Nathan *has* broken the law, he has the right to a fair trial)
* equality rights, which give people the right to be treated fairly no matter what their race, national or ethnic origin, religion, sex, age or mental or physical ability or disability
* official language rights, which include the right to deal with the government in either French or English.

Notwithstanding Clause

When the prime minister and premiers created the *Canadian Charter of Rights and Freedoms* in 1981, they included a special section to act as a safety valve. Its official name is "Section 33(1)" but it's usually called the notwithstanding clause. Ever since it was introduced, it has caused a lot of controversy. It allows the federal or provincial governments to pass laws that go against certain sections of the *Charter*. If the government wants to use the notwithstanding clause it has to pass a law that says clearly that the clause is going to be used for a particular situation. It can only be used for five years at a time. Then it has to be reviewed and discussed again.

The notwithstanding clause has not been used very often. The province of Quebec used it to make sure that all outdoor signs would be in the French language. The clause was also used in Saskatchewan to end a workers' strike.

Canadian citizens have certain rights and freedoms that can't be taken away, even by the notwithstanding clause:

- the right to vote and to stand for office
- mobility rights
- the right to speak whatever language they choose, and to go to school in that language (in certain circumstances)
- the right to be treated equally no matter whether they're a man or a woman.

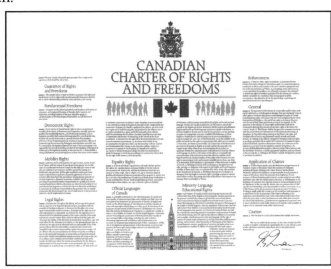

CHAPTER 3

WINNERS & LOSERS

Some people are so keen on running the country that they want to be in the thick of the action, not just *influencing* a political party or an MP, but *being* an MP. Are *you* up to the challenge?

Then please don't wait until election time to start your political career. Start early.

First — I mean, after you turn 14 — join a political party. This kind of party is not about games, dancing and presents. (Sorry, Nathan!) It's a team of people who share the same beliefs about how Canada should be run. There are about a dozen parties in Canada. You can find out what's important to each party by visiting its website, paying attention to the news, and talking to people about it. Join a party that feels right to you — one that shares your own beliefs.

It's easy to join a political party. You just sign up and pay a small fee called dues. The party will be delighted to have you. The more support they have, the better!

Once you've joined up, go to party meetings, rallies and other events in your community. Volunteer to help with events, election campaigns and other work. By the time you're old enough to vote and run for office, you'll be well-known for your good work and enthusiasm.

When election time comes, the party will hold a nomination meeting to choose a candidate. Only one candidate can represent your area in the election, so try to be that person! If you're chosen, you'll represent your party throughout the election and — if your party wins — in the government.

It's important to be a team player. Even if you disagree with something your party believes in, it's wise not to be too vocal about it in public. Choose your party carefully so that you can proudly stand behind its principles! (No, Nathan, not our *school* principal, the *party's* principles. Sheesh.)

You don't have to represent a political party when you run for office. You can run — and maybe win! — as an "independent candidate." Sometimes an MP who has been elected as a member of a particular party later gives up loyalty to that party. When a member votes against the wishes of his or her party — or even makes the more extreme choice of joining a different party or becoming an independent — it's called "crossing the floor."

Nathan says he's going to join the craziest party he can find. There have been a few funny ones in the past. For example, we've had the Absolutely Absurd Party, which promised free Tim Hortons coffee to all Canadians, and the Lemon Party, which wanted to bring "more zest to Canadian politics." For thirty years, we also had the Rhinoceros Party, which wanted to pave the whole province of Manitoba to create the world's biggest parking lot and build a slanted bike path across the whole country so that Canadians could "coast from coast to coast."

Nathan can go ahead and join the craziest party he can find, but I think *you* will choose more carefully and sensibly. After all, you want to *win!*

A Short History of Voting in Canada

1867   When Canada becomes a country, only about 11% of the population has the right to vote. You must be 21 years old, male and a British subject. You must also own some property. (How much? That depends on which province you live in.)

1874   For the first time, secret ballots are used in federal elections. Before this, you had to call out your vote in public. If someone didn't like it, they might beat you up! Meanwhile, many people believe "an election is no place for a woman!"

1900   By the turn of the century, women who own property are allowed to vote in municipal elections, but not in provincial or federal elections.

1916   Women in some provinces win the right to vote.

1918 to 1940   In 1918, women over 21 win the right to vote in federal elections, even those who aren't yet allowed to vote in their own provinces. By 1940, all of the provinces have given women the right to vote.

1947 to 1960   Slowly, other groups win the right to vote: East Indians, Chinese Canadians, Japanese Canadians, Inuit People and Aboriginal People.

1970   The voting age is lowered from 21 to 18.

1982   The *Canadian Charter of Rights and Freedoms* becomes official. It says that every citizen has the right to vote and to stand for office. This means nobody can take away your right to vote, and you can try to be the prime minister! (Uh-oh, so can Nathan.) Still, a few groups had to wait a little longer (see below).

1988   People with mental illnesses, prisoners serving less than two years, and judges in federal courts win the right to vote.

1992   People with physical disabilities win guaranteed access to polling stations.

2002   Prisoners serving two or more years win the right to vote.

Referendums and Plebiscites

Sometimes, instead of voting for a person, we vote yes or no to an important question. This kind of vote is called a referendum or a plebiscite. A separate vote might be held to ask the question or it might be added to the ballot during a regular election. There have been about fifty provincial referendums/plebiscites in Canadian history, but only three federal ones:

1. In 1898 we voted yes to Prohibition: Should it be against the law to drink alcohol?
2. In 1942, during World War II, we voted yes to conscription: Should we allow the government to force people to join the armed forces?
3. In 1992 we voted no to the *Charlottetown Accord*: Should we change Canada's Constitution (in part to give the provinces more control over certain resources, and to recognize Quebec as a distinct society within Canada)?

Do We HAVE To?

Is there a difference between a referendum and a plebiscite? In general, a referendum is legally binding — the government has to do what the voters want — while a plebiscite is *not* binding. But each province has its own rules. The only sure thing about referendums and plebiscites is that "it all depends"!

Election Time

How will you (and Nathan) know it's time to vote? You'll hear about it in the news. And adults will start talking about it — a lot! The prime minister must call an election if:

🍁 five years have passed since the previous election, or

🍁 he or she can't get enough Members of Parliament to vote yes to an important question in the House of Commons — usually something to do with money (this is called losing a vote of confidence).

Sometimes, if the timing is right and the prime minister feels pretty sure of winning, he or she might decide to call an election before five years have passed.

The prime minister chooses a day to be election day. It must be at least 36 days away, and it has to be a Monday. Then he or she goes over to the governor general's house to break the good news. The governor general will — of course — say okay and will end the current session of Parliament. This is called dissolving Parliament. (No, Nathan, that doesn't mean "just add water and stir.")

Start the Countdown!

As soon as the election is announced, everybody starts counting down to Day Zero. There's a lot of work to do. Candidates — like you — plan campaigns and figure out how to win votes. Voters learn about the candidates. Election staff in every community hire and train people to work at polling stations, where the voting will take place, and make sure every adult citizen knows when and where to vote.

Of course, the candidates and political parties can't be in charge of running the election — that would be like letting hockey players referee their own games. So our federal elections are run by an agency called Elections Canada. It's not a part of the government and it doesn't have any connection with a political party. It stays completely neutral, like a good referee. It is responsible for making sure that everyone has a chance to vote and that nobody breaks the election laws. It also keeps track of all the political parties and other groups connected to the election.

The head of Elections Canada is called the chief electoral officer and the person in charge of each district is called a returning officer. (This is not the kind of officer who has a uniform and gun. He or she is just an ordinary person with lots of paperwork to do!)

When you become an election candidate, you'll have to fill out some official forms. Elections Canada will monitor your campaign to make sure you stick to the election rules. For one thing, it'll make sure you don't spend too much money!

Nathan says he doesn't have much money. That's too bad, because it can cost a lot to run an election campaign. You'll have to rent an office and fill it with desks and computers and staff. You'll need signs and stickers and balloons and pins and advertisements. And you'll need to travel around your community to meet voters. If your riding is big, you may have to travel a lot. So you'll need a lot of money.

Luckily, Canadians will pay part of the cost in their taxes. (Every year, each political party receives about $1.75 for each vote it got during the previous election.) You'll try to convince people to give you the rest through fundraising. To keep things fair, there are laws about how much money you can accept and how much you can spend on the election.

Nathan hopes it won't cost more than his allowance. In 2004, the parties in most ridings were allowed to spend 70¢ per voter. This may not sound like much, but it adds up! In 2004, the major parties spent more than $17 million on their campaigns.

Ridings

For voting purposes, our country is divided into 308 parts, which are called electoral districts or ridings. Each riding gets to choose one person to become its Member of Parliament.

Elections Canada keeps track of the population in each district and draws maps to show the boundaries of the ridings. In places where there are a lot of people, like cities, there are more ridings and they are smaller in size. In places where few people live, there are fewer ridings, and they are bigger. (The ridings, I mean. Not the people.) As people move from place to place, the boundaries change and sometimes new ridings are created. There might not always be 308 ridings.

On election day, each riding sets up polling stations where people can go to vote. Each polling station serves about 350 people. That means you won't have to travel very far to vote, no matter where you live.

Nunavut is the biggest riding of all — it covers more than three million square kilometres. The smallest riding is Laurier-Sainte-Marie in Quebec. It covers just nine square kilometres.

3,444,444 Laurier-Sainte-Marie ridings could fit inside 1 Nunavut.

LEARN A LITTLE LINGO

Each MP has a chair in the House of Commons; we say a candidate is trying to win a seat. If your current MP — that is, the person who won the last election — is running again, he or she is called the incumbent. If the only candidate in your riding is you, you'll automatically be declared the winner by acclamation. Congratulations!

Your Campaign

Are you ready to start your election campaign? Here's how:

1. Get some nomination forms from your local Elections Canada office.
2. Hire a team of people to help you get elected — including a campaign manager, an agent and an auditor to take care of the money.
3. To prove that you're serious about being a candidate, deposit $1000 with Elections Canada. As long as you fill out the necessary forms you'll get that money back after the election, even if you don't win.
4. Find at least one hundred people in your riding who want to vote for you.
5. Get them to sign your nomination papers.
6. Take the papers back to Elections Canada by the deadline, which is always 2:00 p.m. on Day 21 of the countdown. Woo-hoo! Now you're an official candidate. Get ready to run!

   While Nathan is busy showing off his new running shoes, let me tell you how to *run* in an election. Yes, you'll be on your feet a lot, but you'll do a lot more speech-making than sprinting. In the old days, candidates stood on a wooden platform, like a stage, when they were giving election speeches. These days, the word platform means the policies and promises you make during your campaign. Each promise (for example, your promise to reduce taxes, or to give more money to farmers) is called a plank. After you give one of your excellent campaign speeches, you might read in the newspaper: *The candidate is running on a platform of lower taxes and increased spending for schools and libraries.*

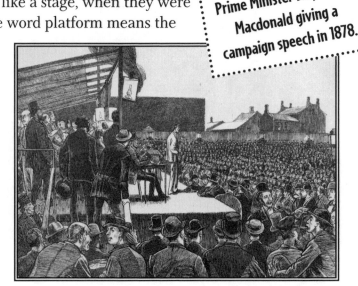

Prime Minister Sir John A. Macdonald giving a campaign speech in 1878.

Hustings

The high platform from which old-time candidates gave their speeches was called the hustings. The word stuck. During your election campaign, when you're busy giving speeches in shopping malls, television studios or school auditoriums, people will say you're "out on the hustings."

Giving speeches is just one way to get people to vote for you. You can also knock on doors and introduce yourself to voters. You can go to crowded places like fairs, parades or sports events, smile a lot and get your picture taken. You can shake hands with people downtown and in malls. This is called mainstreeting. You can give speeches and do radio, TV and newspaper interviews.

While your campaign team is busy flooding your district with flyers, posters and information, you'll be busy attending fancy dinner parties, called fundraisers, to get more money for your campaign. You'll also go to special meetings where voters can meet you and your opponents at the same time. These are called all-candidates meetings. And get ready for at least one debate, where you and your opponents will tackle important issues in public. The voters will watch the debate carefully and make up their minds who to vote for — so be prepared!

Does campaigning sound like a lot of work? It is. David Peterson, who used to be the premier of Ontario, says it's "like running 36 marathons in a row."

Politicians use any opportunity to get out and meet the public. Here, Prime Minister Paul Martin serves hot dogs at a St. Jean Baptiste Day celebration in Quebec.

33

Who Can Vote

Who can vote? In Canada, every adult citizen (except one!) has the right to vote.

Number of people who can vote = about 22,500,000
Number of people who can't vote =   1

Even Nathan agrees: that's a pretty good percentage! The chief electoral officer of Canada has to stay neutral, so he or she can't vote. But everyone else can go to the polls, as long as they're Canadian citizens 18 years of age and over.

Elections Canada keeps a huge computerized list, called the National Register of Voters, of everyone who's eligible to vote. This information comes from the forms adults fill out when they pay income taxes, apply for driver's licences, or deal with other government departments. During the countdown to Day Zero, the people at Elections Canada send voter information cards to all the people on the list.

Even candidates who are running in the election — like you and Nathan — are on the voters' list. (And yes, Nathan, you *can* vote for yourself!)

Votes for Women

If you lived in the 1800s, you'd be shocked by many people's ideas (and they'd be shocked by yours!). Back then, few women went to university. Few had jobs outside their homes. And most people believed that politics and voting were for men only.

In the late 1800s, women began to ask for the right to vote. In Britain and the United States they marched and shouted. Some were arrested. Sometimes violence broke out and people got hurt — a few even died. But in Canada, women fought courageously without violence. They wrote letters and petitions. They gave inspiring speeches. They used logic and even jokes to make their point.

Nellie McClung was one of a number of determined people who pushed for women to get the vote.

It took a long time. Strong women in the Prairie provinces led the way, arguing that they had done just as much to build their communities as men had. During World War I, women ran factories, homes and businesses while men were away fighting. It became harder and harder to argue against their right to vote. In 1916, women in the Prairies won the right to vote in their provincial elections. And in 1918, just as the war was ending, Canadian women won the right to vote in federal elections.

Women's Right to Vote in Canada

January 28, 1916   Manitoba

March 14, 1916   Saskatchewan

April 19, 1916   Alberta

April 5, 1917   British Columbia

April 12, 1917   Ontario

April 26, 1918   Nova Scotia

May 24, 1918   **Canada** (Women could vote in federal elections, even if they couldn't yet vote in their provincial elections.)

April 17, 1919   New Brunswick

May 20, 1919   Yukon

May 3, 1922   Prince Edward Island

April 13, 1925   Newfoundland and Labrador

April 25, 1940   Quebec

June 12, 1951   Northwest Territories

Nunavut   In Nunavut, which was created in 1999, women have always had the vote.

CHAPTER 4

BALLOT TIME

Even though it's so easy to vote, when election day arrives, not everyone will go to the polls. In the past, about 70% of the eligible voters actually voted in our federal elections — and in the 2000 and 2004 elections, only about 60% voted. Some people are concerned about the drop in voter turnout, which is also happening in other countries.

Do the grown-ups in your family vote? Ask them. If they say no, listen patiently to their flimsy excuses. Then clasp your hands under your chin, look up at them with big eyes, and say, "Don't you *care* who runs this country?" If enough of us do this, voter turnout should soon go up.

Voter turnout varies from place to place and election to election. Bad weather can keep people from voting. So can illness or other personal difficulties. People are more likely to vote if:

* they know something about how the government works
* they have a good education and income
* they find it easy to register and to get to the polls
* they live in a community where people don't move very often
* they're older (the older you are, the more likely you are to vote).

People are also more likely to vote if the election contest is close and exciting, and if they strongly prefer a certain political party (or if they strongly *dislike* a candidate).

WHAT IF?

What if one of your biggest fans is going to be on vacation or having an operation on election day? Don't worry. They can still vote for you at one of the advance polls, which are held in the weeks before the official election day. And if voters can't even make it to an advance poll — for example, if they're members of the armed forces or other citizens living far away from home or in another country — they can vote by mail using a special ballot. These early votes will be locked up safely until the polls close on election day. Then all the votes will be counted at the same time.

Soldiers and a wounded patient cast their votes in France while on duty in World War I.

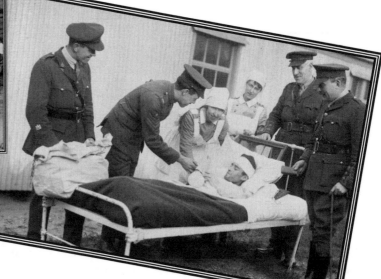

Election Day

Since you and Nathan are candidates, you can go to the polling stations in your home ridings and vote for yourselves. The voter information card you received in the mail will tell you where to go. (*Whoa*, Nathan! I mean which polling station to go to.) The polling station is just a plain ordinary table with two plain ordinary people sitting behind it, and a plain ordinary box with a slot in the top — the ballot box.

Hand over your voter registration card or tell the people who you are. One of them (the poll clerk) will find your name in a computer printout and cross it out. He or she will write your name on the list of people who have voted. The other person (the deputy returning officer) will hand you a folded-up piece of paper with a number and/or set of initials on it. This is your ballot!

Go behind the cardboard screen and open the ballot. You'll see the names of all the candidates in your riding and their political parties. Each name has a white circle next to it. Since you're a candidate, you should stop for a moment and admire your own name on the ballot. Is that *cool*, or what? Then pick up the pencil and mark an X in the circle next to your choice. Don't get fancy with the X. If you decorate the ballot, or draw a happy face, or write anything in the margins, your vote won't count. (Are you listening, Nathan?) So just mark an X and step away from the pencil. Fold up the ballot and give it back to the deputy returning officer. He or she will double-check the number and/or initials (to make sure it's the same ballot you were given) and give it back

Before secret ballots, voters could be bullied into voting for a different candidate.

to you. Drop it in the ballot box. Say thank you. And be thankful that Canada has a secret ballot system, which guarantees that nobody can bribe or bully you into voting a certain way, as they could before 1874.

Maybe you wish you could hang around the polling station on election day, admiring your name on the ballot and shaking hands with voters. But don't do it. There are strict rules against election-day campaigning. After you cast your vote, you should go back to your home or office and wait for the results.

However, you can choose helpers, called scrutineers, who are allowed to visit the polling stations to make sure nobody cheats. If they see something wrong — for example, if they see someone trying to vote twice — they can challenge that person's right to vote, and election staff will investigate the problem.

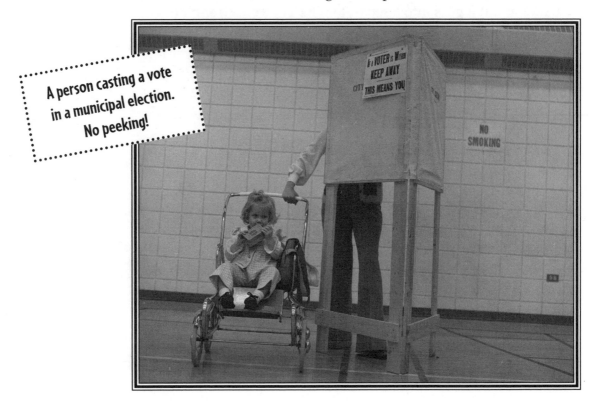

A person casting a vote in a municipal election. No peeking!

Counting Votes

Election day is over. The polls are closed and the doors are locked. Now the fun begins! Don't you wish you could see this part? But you can't. As a candidate, you're at home with your friends, family and campaign workers, waiting for the election results on television and pretending to be calm.

The scrutineers stay inside the polling station with the election staff, who open the ballot box and dump all the ballots onto a table. The only person who can touch the ballots is the deputy returning officer. He or she picks up one ballot at a time, checks to make sure it's official, reads out the name of the candidate who was chosen on that ballot, and places it in the correct pile. If there's anything wrong with a ballot (for example, if the voter wrote anything except an X, or if the X is not inside the circle, or if the voter didn't mark the ballot at all) it goes into a separate pile. The votes from the advance polls are also counted now.

When the counting is finished, the deputy returning officer fills out some official forms. Then all of the ballots go back into the box. It is sealed up again and sent to the returning officer for that riding, who will double-check the paperwork to make sure there were no errors. Elections Canada will keep the box safe in case the ballots need to be recounted.

Right way

Wrong way

Before they go home, the elections staff take an oath to say that the ballot-counting was all official and legal. (No, Nathan — not *that* kind of an oath!) Then the deputy returning officer phones the riding's returning officer to tell him or her the results. The returning officer for each riding reports to the headquarters of your political party and to the television and radio stations. Before you know it, you'll be hearing your name and seeing your picture on TV, along with the number of votes that you and your opponents received. Just look how many votes you got! You won by a landslide.

All of the ballots that went out to the polling stations go back to Elections Canada after voting day.

Unless there's a recount, the returning officer will soon finish the paperwork and tell the chief electoral officer the winner's name. That makes it official. Congratulations! Soon the hard work of running the country begins. But first . . . you celebrate!

(How did Nathan do in his riding? Good grief — he's been elected! What were those voters *thinking?*)

Recount

Nathan wants to know what happens if there's a tie. (Apparently he didn't win by a landslide the way you did!) If there's a tie in a riding or if the results are very close, the ballots can be counted again. If the difference between the top two candidates is less than 1/1000th of the total votes in the riding, the recount will happen automatically. But even if the difference is much bigger than that, any voter or scrutineer or candidate who saw someone cheating or making mistakes during the counting can ask a judge for a judicial recount. If the judge agrees, the recount must take place within four days.

The sealed ballot boxes are brought to a meeting place. Sometimes this is a judge's courtroom. The returning officer and the candidates are also there. The judge checks the seals on the boxes and then opens them, counts the ballots and double-checks the totals for the riding. Then he or she announces the final total. This is the new result for that riding.

If the candidates are *still* tied, there will be a special vote called a by-election in that one riding, and the winner of the by-election will become the riding's MP. In the old days, if the recount ended in a tie, candidates would sometimes flip a coin or draw straws to see who won!

BY-ELECTIONS

There's one other reason for a by-election. Now and then an elected person retires, or leaves his or her job because of illness, or even dies. If this happens between elections, that community won't have anyone to represent it. So a by-election is held to fill the empty seat.

And It's Not Over Yet

Before you head for Ottawa, you'll need to write a report for Elections Canada. You must list all the money you received and spent on your election campaign, and give the list to the returning officer in your riding. Then you'll need to set up a constituency office in your riding. This will be your home base when you're not in Ottawa. From this office you and your staff (NOTE: hire some staff) will:

* meet with your constituents to hear their ideas and concerns
* help people with government problems (like taxes or pensions, passports or visas)
* give newspaper, TV or radio interviews
* study issues that are important to your riding
* receive invitations to ceremonies and special events
* write newsletters and provide other information to your constituents.

As if that's not enough, you must also set up an office in Ottawa. This is called your parliamentary office. You and your staff (NOTE: hire some more staff) will do the same work you do in your constituency office, only more of it. The phones will ring. The letters and e-mail messages will arrive. Documents will pile up. People will drop in. (TIP: Get yourself a nice desk lamp. You'll probably be working late into the evenings.)

CHAPTER 5

ON PARLIAMENT HILL

Majority/Minority

Both you and Nathan will be going to Ottawa. But what teams will you be on when you get there? The team that makes most of the decisions about how to run the country? Or the team that asks tough questions and keeps an eye on the decision makers? That depends how many ridings were won by your party's candidates. Count them up.

Congratulations once again! Since your party won more ridings than the others, your party's leader will become the prime minister. (This happens even if that person didn't win in his or her own riding.) He or she will get to choose the cabinet ministers who run the government departments, and your team will be allowed to propose most of the new laws until the next election. We call this team the government and you're lucky to be on it!

But is the winning party a majority or a minority? If your party won more than half of the seats in the House of Commons it forms what is called a majority government. This is good news for your team. When you propose new ideas in the House of Commons, the other MPs vote either yes or no to them — and since more than half of the MPs belong to your party, you're pretty much guaranteed to win!

If your party won fewer than half the seats in the election (but more seats than any other party) it may still form the government, but this one is called a minority government. This makes things a bit tougher for you. Your party will find it harder to get your new laws accepted. Unless you find ways to co-operate with the other parties, their members can join together and vote no to your ideas.

A minority government doesn't usually stay in office as long as a majority government. It usually ends when the prime minister's team can't get enough votes to pass an important proposal — usually its budget or something else to do with money. This is called a vote of non-confidence. When that happens, the prime minister usually has to call an election, and the whole process of voting would start all over again.

Does your favourite adult know what a vote of non-confidence is? Go ahead and ask. If the adult gets flustered, just sigh and pat him or her gently. Offer to explain it after dinner.

WHICH IS BETTER FOR CANADA?

Some people say that a majority government is a good thing because it's stable, it can get things done without too much arguing, and it usually stays in office for a long time. But some people say it's bad for one party to have so much power. If the government makes a bad decision, the other parties can't easily stop it. Some people think a minority government is better because it forces the government to pay attention to many points of view. There are good arguments for both types of government.

Cabinet

Soon after the election, the prime minister chooses some MPs to join his or her cabinet. This is a real honour and a big responsibility. The cabinet introduces most of the new laws in the House of Commons, and *all* of the laws that spend our tax money. There are about thirty people on this special team of advisors. They're called ministers, and most of them are in charge of government departments, or ministries, like the Ministry of Health or the Ministry of Fisheries and Oceans. If the prime minister chose you to be the Minister of the Environment, you'd be the first person to answer any questions about pollution. You'd run projects to ensure clean air and water, and introduce laws to protect the environment. You'd attend lots of cabinet meetings. As a cabinet minister, you'd support the prime minister's decisions, even if you didn't always agree with them.

Official Opposition

Nathan won't be chosen as a cabinet minister because his political party didn't win the election. The losing parties are called the opposition. Their job is to keep an eye on the government. When your cabinet and prime minister propose new laws, the opposition parties will check them carefully for problems or weaknesses. They won't be shy about pointing them out!

The party that came second in the election is called the Official Opposition, and the head of this party is called the Leader of the Official Opposition. He or she chooses party members to "shadow" the cabinet ministers on your team — that is, to keep you on your

toes. For example, when the prime minister chooses you to be the Environment Minister, the leader of the Opposition will choose a shadow minister to become an expert in environmental issues. That shadow minister will ask tough questions to make sure you work hard. The Opposition's team of shadow ministers is called the shadow cabinet. (Could someone please tell Nathan that shadow ministers don't actually wear capes and speak in spooky voices?)

Taking Your Seat

Think how proud the adults in your life will be as you head for Ottawa! Soon a new session of Parliament will begin, and you and Nathan will take your seats in the House of Commons. The Constitution says that Parliament must meet at least once a year, and you'll probably spend about 27 weeks a year there, from September until June. There will be some breaks so you and Nathan can go back to your home ridings or travel elsewhere on business. If you're lucky, you might even get a vacation. But don't count on it — you're going to be busy!

In your new jobs as MPs, you and Nathan will represent the people in your own ridings, but along with other MPs, you are also responsible to all the people of Canada. MPs vote yes or no to the ideas proposed by the prime minister and cabinet. Your job is to keep an eye on the government and make sure it takes responsibility for its actions and decisions. This is called responsible government. It means the prime minister and cabinet must have the support of the MPs in the House of Commons, who in turn are answerable to the people who elected them.

Tour Time

Finally, you're in Ottawa! Don't get lost. Here's a mini-tour to help you find your way around Parliament Hill.

Step through the gates and walk toward the Parliament Buildings. Soon you'll come to a round fountain with a small flame in the middle of it. The Centennial Flame was lit on Canada's 100th birthday and it has been burning ever since (except for a couple of weeks each year when it's shut down for maintenance). Around the fountain are the symbols of each province and territory. (Yes, Nathan's right! Nunavut is missing from the fountain. That's because it didn't exist in 1967, when the fountain was made.)

As you walk toward the Parliament Buildings you look up, up, up at the tower on the hill. This is the Peace Tower. It was built in memory of the Canadians who died in World War I. It's more than 92 metres tall. The bells inside the tower ring every 15 minutes.

Now climb the steps toward the Centre Block — the heart of Canadian government. The government's work gets done in the West Block (to your left), East Block (to your right) and in various government offices in Ottawa.

Inside the Centre Block, near the foot of the Peace Tower, is the Memorial Chamber. It's a quiet and solemn place. On display are six Books of Remembrance which contain the names of those Canadians who have died in wars. Every morning, one page of each book is turned so that each name will be on display at least once a year. A seventh Book of Remembrance will honour members of the Canadian Forces who have died while serving their country since 1947. (It is still being produced.) You can see all of the pages from the Books of Remembrance on the website of Veterans Affairs Canada.

An Olympic torch bearer stands behind the Centennial Flame, with the Parliament Buildings behind him.

Also in the Centre Block is the Library of Parliament. This is where you and the other members, as well as senators and parliamentary staff, will get the documents and information you need to do your job. The beautiful building, with its high dome, survived the fire that destroyed the rest of the Centre Block in 1916.

Two long corridors stretch east and west from the middle of the building. On one side is the House of Commons. On the other is the Senate. They look similar — but don't get mixed up! MPs are not allowed in the Senate Chamber. When you take your seat for the first time, look down at the carpet. If it's red, you've entered the Senate by mistake. Oops! Tiptoe away!

After most of the Centre Block was destroyed in the fire of 1916, the Victoria Tower was replaced by the Peace Tower (left) to mark the end of the First World War. The only building that survived the fire was the Library (above, at left).

Now and then, you'll be called to the Senate Chamber to watch an important event like the Speech from the Throne — but even then, you'll have to stand behind a brass railing called the bar.

If that doesn't seem fair, consider this: Even the governor general and the Monarch have to stay out of the House of Commons. This tradition started a long time ago.

Since your party's leader is now the prime minister, you'll have your own desk on the government side of the room. The prime minister will sit in the front row, facing the Leader of the Opposition across the middle of the room. The opposition members (including Nathan) will sit near their leader, facing you.

The carpets and chairs in the House of Commons are green. Are you in the right place? Good! Let the fun begin!

Make sure the carpet is green. If it's red, you're in the Senate, not the House of Commons!

FIRE!

One evening in 1916, a shout rang through the Parliament Buildings: "Fire! Everybody out!" People scrambled to escape from the thick black smoke. Some ran. Others jumped from windows. The prime minister crawled to safety almost on his hands and knees. Sections of the roof crashed down. The huge bell fell from the central tower. Then the tower collapsed. Firefighters saved the beautiful library, but the rest of the building was destroyed. Seven people died. How did it start? Probably someone broke the rule against smoking in the Reading Room, and a spark ignited some newspapers. We don't know for sure. But we do know that the fire quickly spread out of control! (And that wasn't the first fire — just 19 years earlier, a fire had damaged the top stories of the West Block.)

Construction crews begin the mammoth job of rebuilding the Parliament Buildings after the disastrous fire.

CHAPTER 6

A NEW SESSION OF PARLIAMENT

Whether it's your first day as an MP or your first day as prime minister, the opening of a new session of Parliament is always exciting. Shine your shoes. Comb your hair. It's time for lights . . . cameras . . . action!

On your first day, you and Nathan will find the other MPs hanging out, chatting or reading in the House of Commons. Suddenly the doors are slammed shut. Three loud knocks are heard, and the Usher of the Black Rod comes in. This impressive-looking person is an official messenger, who has come to summon everyone to the Senate Chamber. Crowd down the hall with your new colleagues. When you get to the Senate, its Speaker will tell you — in fancy language — that you can't yet hear the Speech from the Throne. First, the MPs must choose a Speaker to represent them.

Now, everybody already knew this. It's not news, but it is tradition. So back you go to the House of Commons to elect a Speaker.

Speaker of the House

The Speaker is a kind of chairperson and referee in the House of Commons. He or she also speaks for the House of Commons when it has official business inside or outside Canada. And the Speaker is in charge of the House of Commons employees — all 1500 of them.

The Speaker sits at the front of the room in a big carved chair and makes sure that the day's business gets done smoothly. He or she must be firm and fair in enforcing the rules, no matter whether the rule-breaker is a prime minister or a first-time MP like you and you-know-who. The Speaker also makes decisions about tricky and complicated rules of debate. This can sometimes be difficult if the members are forcefully debating an issue!

Every question in the House of Commons must be addressed to the Speaker.

Wrong way: What are you talking about?

Right way: Mr. Speaker, what is the Honourable Member talking about?

The Speaker isn't usually allowed to vote in the House of Commons, but if there's a tie, the Speaker gets to break it. He or she tries to cast the deciding vote in a way that will keep the debate going as long as possible. During a single month in 2005, the Speaker broke two ties. He voted once in favour of the opposition and once in favour of the government. In each case, his vote kept the debate going. The Senate also has a Speaker, appointed by the governor general on the advice of the prime minister.

Don't Shoot the Messenger!

When a new Speaker is elected, don't be startled to see this strange tradition: a couple of members will grab that person and drag him or her to the Speaker's chair, with the Speaker resisting all the way! The tradition started many hundreds of years ago in Britain, when the Speaker sometimes had to give bad news to the king or queen. Once in a while, a monarch took revenge by cutting off the Speaker's head!

Speech from the Throne

After the new Speaker is elected, it's time for
the Speech from the Throne.
With a swirl of pageantry, the
governor general enters the
Senate Chamber and sits on the
throne. You and Nathan don't
see this part, because you're in
the House of Commons with the
other MPs. Once again you hear
bang-bang-bang on the door. Once
again it's the Usher of the Black
Rod. Walk down the hallway to the
Senate Chamber.

Governor General Adrienne
Clarkson about to read the
Speech from the Throne in
February 2004.

Black Rod

The Black Rod, the ceremonial weapon used to bang on the door
of the House of Commons when MPs are invited to the Senate, is
inscribed with the words *Evil to the one who thinks evil.* It's carried
by an official messenger called the Usher of the Black Rod. Like
many of our traditions, this one started in Britain before the time
of Shakespeare. It's been going on ever since.

Ask your favourite grandparent about the Usher of the Black Rod.
If he or she looks confused, just shake your head and walk away.

The Chamber is packed with senators, visitors and all nine of
the Supreme Court judges in their red robes with white fur collars.
It's a very fancy occasion.

Your new Speaker exchanges some promises with the Speaker
of the Senate. Then the governor general reads the Throne Speech,
partly in French and partly in English. The ideas in the speech have
been put together by the government and cabinet ministers, and it
has been written by the staff in the Prime Minister's Office (PMO).

It tells what the government thinks about how Canada is doing, and what types of problems seem most important at the moment. It gives a general idea of the kinds of laws the government plans to introduce during the new session of Parliament.

I hope you wore comfortable shoes! The speech usually lasts about an hour.

The Address Debate

After the Throne Speech has been read, you and the other MPs can roll up your sleeves and get to work. It's time to start debating, and the topic is the Address in Reply to the Speech from the Throne. The first day of this debate is called Leaders' Day, and the first speaker is the Leader of the Opposition. The prime minister speaks next. The debate goes back and forth for six days and covers most of the important ideas from the Throne Speech. You'll hammer out a general idea about where this session of Parliament is going, and what it hopes to do.

Soon Nathan will get tired of playing with his headphones and asking for fresh pencils, and everyone can settle down to work.

DON'T CLAP

Visitors to the House of Commons sit in balconies called galleries around the edges of the room. No noise or applause is allowed there — even if the MPs themselves are shouting or clapping.
A visitor who breaks the rules can be shushed or even asked to leave.

CHAPTER 7

A DAY IN THE HOUSE OF COMMONS

A session of Parliament is like a school semester. It usually runs from September until June. A schedule tells where you need to be on each day of the week and what subject to study during each period. Before long, you and Nathan will know the routine by heart.

Caucus

Check your schedule. If today is a Wednesday, don't go to the House of Commons until 2:00. Wednesday mornings are for caucus meetings. You and the other members of your political party — senators and MPs together — will meet in private to talk about your party's strategy and decide how to respond to questions that are being debated in the House. This is the only place where your team can hash out disagreements and ask your colleagues to explain their actions. In public, you have to vote yes to ideas that your party supports. If you don't, you could be disciplined. If you're a cabinet minister, you might even have to resign. So caucus meetings are a good place to say what you really think.

Meanwhile, you may hear funny noises coming from the room down the hall where Nathan's party is holding its caucus meeting. Just roll your eyes and walk on by.

Get ready ... Get set ...

Every morning the Speaker, clerks and security staff walk together down the corridor on their way to the House of Commons. This is called The Speaker's Parade.

The daily Speaker's Parade approaching the House of Commons. Note the mace — and the hats!

When the Speaker enters the House of Commons, please stand up until he or she sits in the big chair and the Sergeant-at-Arms places a ceremonial golden staff called the mace on the table. Nathan thinks mace is a weapon, like pepper spray. But it's not. It represents the government's authority to run the country and make new laws. In fact, the House can't meet without it. Long ago, before guns or pepper spray, maces *were* weapons — they were clubs, used for whacking people. Nowadays in Parliament, the mace sits in a special holder when the Speaker is in the House of Commons, pointing toward the prime minister's party. When the Speaker leaves the House, the mace is moved to a set of brackets underneath the table.

Now you can sit down. After a prayer and some announcements, the day's business begins.

DON'T TOUCH THE MACE!

One time an MP lost his temper over a decision the prime minister had made. He grabbed the mace from the table and shook it at the Speaker, saying, "Canadians no longer live in a democracy." By grabbing the mace, which is a symbol of Parliament's power, the MP had challenged the government's authority. The other MPs voted to suspend him from the House. Only after he apologized was he allowed back in.

57

What if you take your seat in the House of Commons and suddenly find that you're thirsty? What if you suddenly need to send a message to someone? Don't worry — just ask a page. (Nathan figured out that particular parliamentary tradition in about one minute flat.) These young people, who act as messengers and helpers for the MPs, are stationed near the Speaker's chair while the House is in session. In all, there are 40 of them. They're university students who work part-time in the House, and when they aren't serving the Speaker, MPs and other staff, they handle other duties. They're almost as busy as you are — especially with Nathan to look after!

As you look around the House of Commons you'll also notice the cameras — smile, you're on TV! Canadians were the first in the world to be able to watch their government's proceedings on television, beginning in 1977. Since 1995 we've also been able to click our way to the action on the Web.

Cameras aren't the only way to find out what's going on in Parliament. You can also keep informed by reading *Hansard*. All of the House of Commons proceedings are recorded on tape. Every day, specially trained staff listen to the tapes and type every word into a computer. By 9:00 a.m. you can read the previous day's debates in English or French, on paper or on-line.

The official name for this record is *The Debates of the House of Commons*, but most people call it *Hansard* because in the 1880s the printer who recorded the debates of the British parliament was T. C. Hansard. (Nathan wants to know why he didn't just post them on the Web. Good grief!)

Another team of specialists also works in the House of Commons: the interpreters. They translate all the speeches into English and French as soon as the words are spoken. Members and visitors can hear the translation through headphones at their seats.

. . . Go!

Okay. The Speaker is seated, the public are in their seats in the visitors' galleries, and everyone's ready to work (even Nathan). Let the day begin!

1. Routine Proceedings

You'll start the day by listening to certain kinds of business. Maybe a committee will give a report on something its members have studied. Maybe an MP will talk about a petition from his or her constituents. Maybe someone will introduce a new bill or an idea to be debated. This part of the day is called routine proceedings. It's very . . . routine.

2. Government Orders

Next, the prime minister's team gets the spotlight. During government orders they can introduce new ideas, questions, bills or proposals.

3. Members' Statements

Do you have something to say? Here's your big chance. During a 15-minute session each day, MPs are invited to speak about matters of importance to them. If you choose to speak up, be brief! Your speech can only be one minute long. It does have to be work-related — you can't get up and announce that it's your birthday or that your sister is selling Girl Guide cookies. Also — not that you would do this, of course — you can't use bad language, or attack anyone, or criticize a judge or a court decision. Congratulatory messages and recitations of poetry are also out. If you don't use your minute properly, the Speaker may tell you to resume your seat. How embarrassing. But if you've got something worthwhile to say, do it now!

4. Question Period

The most famous (and fun) part of the day is called Question Period. Its official name is Oral Questions. It lasts for 45 minutes, and it can get pretty lively. During Question Period, opposition MPs get to ask cabinet ministers about the government's plans, actions and policies. They force the government to take responsibility for its decisions.

These questions are supposed to be about urgent matters, so Nathan won't be allowed to ask anything trivial, thank goodness. And he won't be allowed to go on and on, or ask something very technical. If he does, the Speaker will stop him. But if he asks a good question he might spark a lively debate or put pressure on the government to take care of an important issue. If Nathan thinks the answer he got was too flimsy, he can ask it again in writing. A cabinet minister or staff member will answer him during the adjournment proceedings at the end of the day.

John G. Diefenbaker, as an MP and later as prime minister, was known for his fiery speeches and forceful debate, both in the House and on the campaign trail.

RULES OF QUESTION PERIOD

Make sure your question is brief and that you're really asking for information — don't offer statements, arguments or personal opinions. Your question should be about something important and fairly urgent, and it should be addressed to the appropriate minister. Don't use "what if?" questions or ask the minister to give an opinion. Don't repeat a question that has already been answered that day, and don't ask about anything that's being discussed in a court of law or anything the minister has said outside the House of Commons. If you ask just the right question, or start a lively discussion, you might end up on the evening news!

5. Private Members' Business

Most new laws start out as government bills. They're introduced by cabinet ministers. But during private members' business, other MPs are allowed to introduce bills. So many MPs want to do this that a draw is held at the beginning of each new session of Parliament to decide who will go first. In the past, not many private members' bills actually became laws, and the ones that did were not about very controversial subjects. For example, one private member's bill dealt with the subject of National Organ Donor Week. But in 2003 the rules changed, and now there's a better chance that you can turn an important idea into law.

Did your name get chosen in the lucky draw? Do you have a good idea? Go for it! Just be aware that if your bill requires the spending of public money (taxes) you'll have to ask a cabinet minister to back up your proposal.

Committees

One of the most important and time-consuming parts of your job as an MP is your committee work. At the beginning of the new session of Parliament, you'll get appointed to two or more committees. So will Nathan. Each of you will spend between 6 and 40 hours a week in committee meetings. There are usually about 20 permanent committees, called standing committees. (Yes, Nathan, you can sit down during the meetings.) They deal with things like agriculture, transportation and so on. There are also temporary committees that study particular issues or bills.

Types of Committees

- 🍁 Committees of the Whole include the entire membership of the House of Commons
- 🍁 Joint Committees include both senators and MPs

- Legislative Committees are temporary committees that examine bills in detail
- Special Committees study important issues in detail; they are sometimes called task forces
- Standing Committees study subjects that are always important, such as health, cities, the environment, etc.

Naming

In the House of Commons you should refer to MPs by the riding they represent, like this: "The Honourable Member for Ottawa Centre." This is a sign of respect. One of the most serious ways for the Speaker to discipline an MP is to name him or her. (Nathan, are you paying attention to this part?)

The Speaker might name someone for using rude language, interrupting, repeating or talking off-topic, acting out or refusing to obey the rules. The Speaker usually warns the person first, and this is usually enough to stop the behaviour. But if the disturbance continues, the MPs can vote to suspend the rule-breaker. If that happens, the member is taken out of the House of Commons by the Sergeant-at-Arms. The rule-breaker can be suspended for one day or longer, depending on the situation. Usually, he or she apologizes and is allowed back into the house right away.

Behind the Scenes

It takes more than MPs and senators to keep things running on Parliament Hill. Behind the scenes, more than 1700 staff members are busy advising, researching, writing documents and doing hundreds of other tasks. Some of them give legal advice or help with research or procedures. Others work with computers, finances, information or printing. Still others take care of the grounds, buildings and security. And then there are the staff who hire, train and manage all these employees! They all help run the country too.

Government Watchdogs

Who keeps an eye on the government? How do Canadians know what the PM and MPs are up to? Certain people and organizations are responsible for keeping the government accountable to Canadians. We often call them "government watchdogs."

1. Media

Ordinary Canadians can watch the news, listen to the radio, or read newspapers to find out what the government is doing. Reporters (sometimes called "the press" or "the media") have a special role in telling Canadians about the government's activities. Sometimes reporters investigate and research things that might not make the government look good. For this reason, the *Canadian Charter of Rights and Freedoms* protects the freedom of the press. It prevents the government from interfering with the work of journalists, even those who work for government agencies like the CBC.

2. Agents of Parliament

Several agents of Parliament are responsible for making sure the government stays fair and does a good job for Canadians. These watchdogs include:

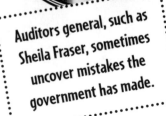

* the chief electoral officer
* the privacy commissioner, who protects your right to know what information the government collects about you, and why
* the information commissioner, who protects your right to see that information
* the commissioner of official languages, who makes sure all federal information and services are available in both of Canada's official languages: English and French.
* the auditor general, who makes sure Canadians are getting good value for the money the government spends on their behalf.

Auditors general, such as Sheila Fraser, sometimes uncover mistakes the government has made.

3. Other Watchdogs

Other watchdogs include bodies like the Canadian Human Rights Commission or provincial ombudsmen. These people or agencies independently review and investigate cases where people feel they have been unfairly treated by a government agency.

One of the most important watchdogs is the public — you and me! The government sometimes makes decisions based on public opinion, so if a lot of people feel strongly about an issue, they can influence the way the government behaves. For example, in 2003 the United States asked Canada to help fight a war in Iraq. Many Canadians were against this idea, and they made their views known to the government. They protested in many Canadian cities. Over a hundred thousand people protested in Montreal alone. The prime minister got the message. He told the Americans no.

Who runs this country, anyway? *We* do! The government's job is to listen to us. *Our* job is to speak up.

Nathan says he enjoys being a watchdog. (No kibble required!)

The "Raging Grannies" dress up in wild clothes to attract attention when they protest for peace, while other citizens might join marches. As citizens, we have an obligation to voice our opinions on important issues.

CHAPTER 8

IT'S THE LAW!

How to Introduce a Bill

A bill is a proposal or plan for a new law. One of your most important jobs as an MP is to study, discuss and amend (change) bills and to vote on them in the House of Commons. Every bill that becomes a law has gone through this careful process in both the House of Commons and the Senate. Both Houses must vote yes before a bill can become a law.

New bills are usually proposed and introduced by cabinet ministers. But bills can also be introduced by private members or in the Senate, as long as they don't involve public money. Only cabinet ministers can propose bills to collect or spend our taxes.

Which bills are being considered right now? You can see them on the Parliament of Canada Web site. Just click on *Bills*.

If you want to impress your family, simply mention one of these at the dinner table, like this: "I understand that Bill C-145 was introduced in the House of Commons today. Please pass the milk . . ."

Step 1: First Reading

Bills usually go through the same steps in both the House of Commons and the Senate. The bill is introduced during the step called First Reading. You don't debate it yet. The Speaker says, "When shall the bill be read a second time?" Usually the answer is "At the next sitting of the House."

If the bill is being introduced in the House of Commons, it gets a special number beginning with C — for example, C-103. If it's being introduced in the Senate, it begins with S — for example, S-104. (If it's introduced by Nathan, it begins with N. No, not really. I'm just kidding. Hahaha.) Then the text of the bill is sent to the printer. If it's a tax bill or something to do with spending public money, it's tied with a green ribbon.

Step 2: Second Reading

When the day comes for the Second Reading, please pay attention. This is an important step. You and the other MPs debate the idea behind the bill — the principle of the bill. You discuss whether the bill is good policy. You don't talk about the details. You just try to decide whether the bill will make a good law.

If you don't want to talk about the bill now, you can set it aside until the next session of Parliament. This is called the six-months' hoist. (Wouldn't it be great if you could get a six-months' hoist on your homework assignment? Just tell the teacher you'll hand it in next term!)

Step 3: Committee Stage

Now it's time to look at the details. A committee — usually one of the standing committees — studies the bill paragraph by paragraph, or clause by clause. Experts and other members of the public may appear before the committee as witnesses. Any member of the committee can suggest changes, so if you see a clause you don't like, speak up! Finally, the committee writes a report to tell the other MPs what they think about the bill.

Step 4: Report Stage

The committee reports back to the House of Commons with its advice: to accept the bill, or to accept it with certain changes, or to reject it. Now the other MPs get a chance to suggest changes that didn't get proposed by the committee. They vote yes or no to each of these changes. Then the bill goes to its Third Reading.

Step 5: Third Reading

The bill comes back to the House one more time. No changes are allowed at this stage. It's time to vote! Will the bill become a law or not? In the halls and offices all over Parliament Hill, bells begin to ring with a *ping-ping-ping* sound. They're calling you and Nathan to the House of Commons — you've got 15 minutes to get to your seats. At least 20 MPs must be in their seats before the vote can take place. This minimum number is called a quorum, and it hasn't changed since 1867. If there isn't a quorum, the vote can't take place.

Take your seat. The Speaker will remind you and the other MPs what you're voting for. Then he or she will ask, "Is it the pleasure of the House to adopt the motion?" If nobody says no, the bill is passed unanimously. If someone says no or nay the Speaker will take a voice vote. The MPs in favour of the bill will say yea. (Pronounce it yay, not yeah . . . and Nathan, don't say it like this: *YAAAY!*) Those who are against it will say nay. If there are more yeas than nays, the bill passes.

WHERE'S THE WHIP?

Each political party chooses one MP to be the party's whip. Along with other duties, the whip also has to make sure there are enough party members in the House of Commons when it's time to vote.

Step 6: Second House

Just when you think a bill has become law, it hasn't. Not yet. The Senate still has to approve it (and vice-versa: if a bill starts in the Senate, it can't become law until the House of Commons approves it). Now the bill gets sent to the Senate, where it goes through the same stages as it did in the House: First Reading, Second Reading, Committee Stage, Report Stage and Third Reading. If the senators want to amend the bill, they can send a message to the House of Commons, and if the House of Commons wants to amend the amendment, they can send a message back. The bill can't become law until both houses have approved it in identical form.

Step 7: Royal Assent

Time for another ceremony! The bill won't really, truly become law until the Monarch (or the governor general, who represents the Monarch . . . or a judge or deputy who represents the governor general) gives it royal assent. Assent means "saying yes." Royal assent has never been refused in Canada. Usually the governor general writes his or her signature on the bill to show that it has received royal approval. But twice a year a traditional ceremony is used.

The ceremony is like the Throne Speech, but a lot shorter. You and the other MPs can watch from the bar of the Senate while some formal words are spoken. Then the title of the bill is read aloud. The governor general nods. One clerk announces that the bill has received assent and another clerk thanks you and your colleagues. That's all! With one little nod, the bill has become a law.

His Majesty King George VI and Queen Elizabeth in our Senate Chamber to give royal assent to bills.

A FUNNY LITTLE RULE

When you're in the House of Commons, you must not say the word **Senate** (and senators must not say **the House of Commons**). If you want to say something about the other House, you should say **The Other Place** instead, like this: The bill has been sent to **The Other Place**. (Don't wink.)

Consensus Government

Nunavut and the Northwest Territories have a special sort of government called a consensus government. In this process, Aboriginal traditions have been mixed with British and Canadian traditions to make a system that is unique in the world. There are no political parties — each candidate runs as an independent. After the election, the winners choose their own Speaker, premier and cabinet by secret ballot. The rest of the members act as the opposition. When it's time to make a decision, everyone is expected to speak up, especially those who disagree. In consensus government, members must be very patient and respect differences of opinion. No decision is made until everyone has had a chance to talk, and no action is taken unless a majority of members agree with it.

What Happens in Some Other Countries?

Forms of government vary around the world. Here are some interesting facts you can use to try to stump your teacher:

❦ In Australia (and 22 other countries) you *have* to vote — you might have to pay a fine if you don't! Voter turnout is usually more than 90%.

❦ In Bosnia and Herzegovina the people elect three presidents. Every eight months they trade places so each of them gets a chance to be the President of the Presidency.

❦ In India, during a 1996 election, one riding had 1033 candidates running for the same seat. The ballot was in the form of a booklet!

❦ The smallest polling station in Hong Kong is a village office and community centre on Lantau Island. In September 2004, it had 35 voters.

❦ The president of the United States always serves for four years. The U.S. election always takes place in a year that can be divided evenly by the number 4 — for example, 2008, 2012, 2016, etc.

❦ When voters in the Ukraine realized that there had been cheating and other problems in their country's 2004 election, they protested in the streets for 17 days until a new election was called. They waved orange flags representing their political party, so the protest was called the Orange Revolution. In the repeat election, a different candidate was chosen.

CHAPTER 9

THAT'S A WRAP!

Vacation Time (The End of a Session of Parliament)

After a busy session of Parliament, you'll be ready for a break. Is it vacation time yet?

A session of Parliament can last anywhere from a few days to a few years. Sometimes it ends because an election has been called. Other times it ends because both the House of Commons and the Senate have finished their business and are ready to take a break. This break between sessions is called prorogation. (After a long word like that, Nathan *needs* a break.)

The prime minister decides when to have this break, and asks the governor general to declare that the session has been prorogued. The prime minister and cabinet ministers remain in office, but everyone takes a sort of vacation until the next session of Parliament begins. If MPs or senators are still discussing a bill when prorogation happens, they must stop. We say the bill *died on the Order Paper.*

If the government wants to continue making that new law, it can be introduced again — as a new bill — at the beginning of the next session. The MPs (or senators, if it's a Senate bill) can take a vote to see if they want to pick up where they left off.

The next session must begin within one year. In the meantime, welcome to your vacation — at least, your vacation from the House of Commons. There will be plenty of work waiting for you back home in your riding!

CONCLUSION

(Nathan, come back! I didn't mean "welcome to your *school* vacation." I was talking about Parliament!) But this *is* the end of our presentation, and it *is* time for recess. So we thank our audience very much for their kind applause. We're glad you liked our show. We hope you'll take our advice and get yourself elected sometime soon. See you on Parliament Hill!

PHOTO CREDITS

The publisher wishes to thank the following for permission to reprint photographs.

Cover photograph (adapted), courtesy of the Library of Parliament/Bibliothèque du Parlement, Mone's Photography
Cover illustration by Lorna Bennett

p. 2: Parliament Buildings from Russell House. Elihu Spencer/Library and Archives Canada, PA-147742
p. 3 (left): keith levit photography/Firstlight, FLR1713888-53
p. 3 (right): Provincial Buildings, Halifax, N.S. Isaac Parrish/Library and Archives Canada, C-008555
p. 9: © The Supreme Court of Canada; photograph by Philippe Landreville
p. 10: Oxford University vs. Switzerland hockey game. Lester B. Pearson is at right front; Switzerland, ca. 1922-1923. Library and Archives Canada, PA-119892
p. 12: Office of the Secretary to the Governor General of Canada 2005; reproduced with the permission of the Minister of Public Works and Government Services 2005
p. 13: Paul Chiasson/Canadian Press/CP, C XPCH107
p. 17: Parliament Buildings, original Centre Block with the Victoria Tower, completed 1878. D.A. McLaughlin/Library and Archives Canada, C-003760
p. 18: George P. Roberts/Library and Archives Canada, C-000733
p. 19: James Ashfield, Photograph of painting by Robert Harris, entitled *Conference at Quebec in October 1864, to Settle the Basis of A [sic] Union of the British North American Provinces,* Library and Archives Canada, C-002149
p. 20: Robert Cooper/Library and Archives Canada, PA-141503
p. 21: Courtesy of the Assembly of First Nations/National Indian Brotherhood
p. 23: Department of Canadian Heritage. Reproduced with the permission of the Minister of Public Works and Government Services Canada, 2005
p. 32: *The great meeting in the amphitheatre, 1878,* from *Canadian Illustrated News,* Aug. 31, 1878, Library and Archives Canada, C-068193
p. 33: Courtesy of the Prime Minister's Office, photo by Dave Chan, PMO
p. 34: Cyril Jessop/Library and Archives Canada, PA-030212
p. 37 (left): Canadians voting in the field for the British Columbia Elections, France. Sept. 1916. W. I. Castle/Canada. Dept. of National Defence/Library and Archives Canada, PA-000554
p. 37 (right): Wounded Canadian soldiers voting at a Canadian hospital, Arras, France, Oct. 1918. William Rider-Rider/Dept. of National Defence/Library and Archives Canada, PA-003488

p. 38: *An election during the struggle of [sic] responsible Government,* by Charles William Jefferys. Library and Archives Canada, C-073707, and the C. W. Jefferys Estate
p. 39: Glenbow Archives, NA-2864-26228
p. 41: Courtesy of Elections Canada
p. 46: Interior of the House of Commons, Parliament Buildings. D.A. McLaughlin/Library and Archives Canada C-003913
p. 48: Olympic torch bearer on Parliament Hill, Ottawa. Fotosearch 484010
p. 49 (left): (Detail), courtesy of the Library of Parliament/Bibliothèque du Parlement, Mone's Photography
p. 49 (right): View of the Library of Parliament and the rear of the Centre Block; Parliament Buildings, Ottawa, Ont. 1880. Samuel McLaughlin/Library and Archives Canada, PA-138522
p. 50: Commons Chamber, Parliament Buildings, Interior, House of Commons, Ottawa, 1880. James Esson/Library and Archives Canada, C-003874
p. 51: Reconstruction of Centre Block, Parliament Buildings, 15 Aug., 1916, DPW/Library and Archives Canada, PA-130624
p. 54: Photography by Sgt Éric Jolin, Rideau Hall
p. 57: Courtesy of the House of Commons
p. 60: John G. Diefenbaker, M.P., speaking in the House of Commons, Ottawa, Ont. 1948. Louis Jacques/Library and Archives Canada, C-080883
p. 64: Office of the Auditor General of Canada. Reproduced with the permission of the Minister of Public Works and Government Services, 2005
p. 65: Courtesy of the Ottawa Raging Grannies
p. 70: H.M. King George VI and Queen Elizabeth in the Senate Chamber giving Royal Assent to Bills, Ottawa, Ont. 1939. National Film Board of Canada/Photothèque/Library and Archives Canada, C-033278